DEMCO

NEW LOOK

Beginnings
and Endings

Henry Pluckrose
Photography by Steve Shott

Children's Press
A Division of Grolier Publishing
New York • London • Hong Kong • Sydney
Danbury, Connecticut

Yuma Co. Library Dist.
350 3rd Ave.
Yuma, AZ 85364
928-782-1871
www.yumalibrary.org

Let's begin with a thought.
Most things have a beginning.
Each day begins with a sunrise ...

and ends with a sunset,
the beginning of the night.

Spring is the season
when new life begins.

Winter is the season when some life comes to an end. The old year ends in winter.

"Start" means the same as "begin."
We do not start school
when we are grown up ...

or go to work
when we are
very young.

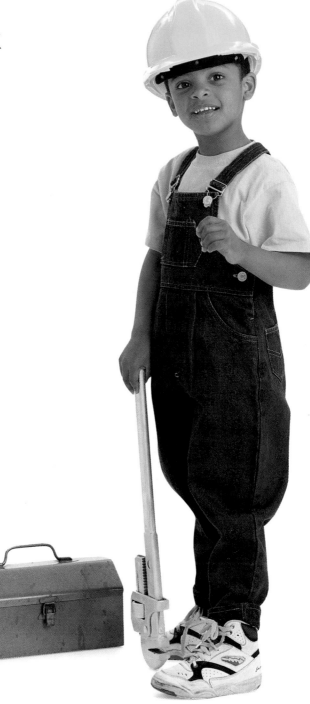

Beginnings are
important.
We do not begin
to dress
by putting on
our shoes –
and then
our socks.

If we did
we might end up
looking like this!

9

Think about it.
Many things have ends.
Hair ...

coils of rope ...

11

and even balls of yarn.

13

Sometimes an end has a particular use. Why do we sharpen only one end of a pencil?

Which end of the
spoon do you
use to eat
your food?

Some things have ends
that look the same ...

even though they
may face in
different directions.

Sometimes an end is a beginning.
This train ends its journey at the station.

When it starts again, it is the beginning of a new journey.

A road may come to the end.
But it could be the beginning of a meadow.

This is the end of the land.
It is also the beginning of the sea.

Some things have
no beginning
and no end –
like this bicycle
chain . . .

and this
necklace.

But not books! The book you are reading had a beginning and now it has an end.

Index

bicycle chains 22
books 24
directions 17
dressing 8–9
food 15
hair 10
journeys 18–19
land 21
looking the same 16
meadows 20
necklaces 23

night 3
pencils 14
roads 20
rope 11
school 6
sea 21
seasons 4–5
shoes 8
socks 8
spoons 15
spring 4

sunrises 2
sunsets 3
trains 18
winter 5
wood 12
work 7
yarn 13
years 5

About this book

Children view the world from a different eye level to adults yet spend their formative years in an environment specifically created for adults. This book, along with its companions in the series, is a visual exploration of everyday life from the child's viewpoint. The photographs and the text encourage talk and personal discovery – both vital elements in the learning process. — Henry Pluckrose

About the author

Henry Pluckrose is a very well known educationalist and respected author of many information books for young people. He is a former primary school headmaster who is now an educational consultant for different organizations worldwide.

© 1996 Watts Books
First American Edition
© 1996 by Children's Press
A Division of Grolier Publishing
Sherman Turnpike
Danbury, Connecticut 06816
All rights reserved.
Printed in Malaysia.
Published simultaneously in Canada.
1 2 3 4 5 R 99 98 97 96 95 94

Library of Congress Cataloging-in-Publication Data

Pluckrose, Henry Arthur.
   Beginnings and Endings / by Henry Pluckrose ;
   illustrated by Steve Shott.
      p. cm. -- (New Look)
   ISBN 0 516-08236-1
      1. Seriation (Psychology)--Juvenile literature. 2.
Perception--Juvenile literature.[1. Perception.]
   I. Shott, Steve. ill. II. Title. III. Series.
   BF445.P57 1995
   428.1--dc20
                                                   94-44515
                                                   CIP AC